BATH

BROAD STREET (W) *c*. 1908. On the left is the end of Bladud's Buildings, now fitted with a shop front and used as a hair salon. The corner with the elegant street light has since been set back. On the right is part of the York House Hotel, as well as Fuller & Hick's wine shop and cellars, which later became the Royal York Tavern. It too has closed along with the hotel and both are in a dreadful state of disrepair.

Previous page: EMPIRE HOTEL, ORANGE GROVE (GA) 1915. Its design by Charles Edward Davis, caused as great a controversy then as it has lately. The foundation stone was laid on 7 December 1899 and it opened on 28 November 1901. It has recently been converted to flats, following restoration. The awnings have now gone and alterations have been made to the top of the building.

IMAGES OF ENGLAND

BATH

PAUL DE'ATH

TEMPUS

First published 1995
Reprinted 1998, 1999, 2007

Tempus Publishing
Cirencester Road, Chalford,
Stroud, Gloucestershire, GL6 8PE
www.tempus-publishing.com

Tempus Publishing is an imprint of NPI Media Group

British Library Cataloguing in Publication Data.
A catalogue record for this book is available from the British Library.

ISBN 978 0 7524 0127 0

Typesetting and origination by NPI Media Group
Printed in Great Britain

Front cover illustration: The residents of South View Road pose for the camera during the celebration of Queen Victoria's Diamond Jubilee. (See page 92)

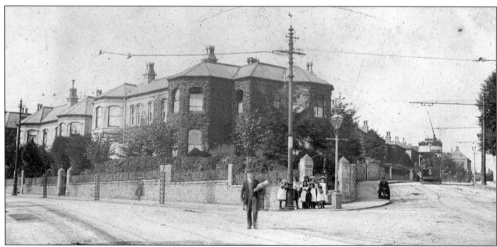

NEWBRIDGE ROAD AND NEWBRIDGE HILL 1905. A group of children pose for the camera at the junction of the two roads to Bristol.

Contents page: RUSTIC BRIDGE, VICTORIA PARK (V) c. 1915. A popular place for watching the ducks swimming in the lake. The bridge had not long replaced an earlier timber structure with a central pier. Nowadays it has stone parapets with a timber lattice construction in between.

Contents

WATCHMAN'S BOX, NORFOLK CRESCENT (C) 1905. This is situated opposite the crescent and was erected in 1793. The sign above the doorway explaining that it was restored by the Urban Sanitary Authority in 1896 has been removed, as have the railings and the lamp column.

Acknowledgements

This book is dedicated to the late Peter Jones, whose inspiration initiated my collection of post cards and photographs of the Bath area.

I have also been aided by my parents who have been pestered with many questions concerning the contents of this book. I am grateful to Anthony and Philip Wooster for their assistance with many aspects relating to the various post cards displayed here and for the travelling to the many fairs around the country. I am indebted to the staff of the Bath Record Office, the Bath Reference Library, to Marek Lewcun and David Pollard for their wealth of information. Also to Peter Lincoln and John Rowe for constantly finding new quality material over the years to add to my collection. Finally to Mr Parr at Ferry Cottage, Warleigh and Mr Salter at Englishcombe Post Office for their interest and on the spot information.

WELLS ROAD AND BLOOMFIELD ROAD (W) *c.* 1904. Looking away from Bath, the Wells Road, now the Wellsway, rises to the left. Bloomfield Road and Elm Place are on the right. In the foreground the road is now split into a dual carriageway. The lamp at the junction has gone and is today occupied by a row of telephone kiosks.

Introduction

My interest in old photographs and post cards of the local area began with Bathford, the village I grew up in. It was only upon meeting Peter Jones that I was able to appreciate the extent of local post cards that were published. Not long afterwards I started to expand my horizons to some of the other villages nearby, later accumulating views from the city as well. Unfortunately, over the last couple of years it has become increasingly difficult to obtain good quality photographic post cards of the area.

On compiling this book I decided that it would be advisable to visit and compare all the views in the publication with the present day. This took quite a while, but was very entertaining. The book has been set out so that if anyone wanted to, they could follow its course on foot. There are many different ways in which this could be achieved, but I hope that the final arrangement proves acceptable.

I have often thought that if it was ever possible to travel back in time to see the city at its best, then I would choose to return to about 1850. Georgian Bath by this time was complete and the large expanse of Victorian suburbs had not yet begun to cover the landscape. The last chance to see the city before the destruction began was in the 1930s. The bombing of the city during the Second World War and subsequent wholesale demolition of blocks of buildings have brought to an end an era. The often alien replacements have left the city in many places a shadow of its former self.

Travelling about the locality, I found several features that stood out time and time again. Firstly, and not too surprisingly, not one picture in this book is identical today, although some do come very close. Due to the need for iron during the Second World War many railings, wherever they were located, subject to personal safety, were cut down. I have only seen a few exceptions to this and these were presumably oversights. The general condition of boundary walls in rural areas leaves a lot to be desired, but at least now, many of the houses have had the benefit of being cleaned of accumulated years of grime. If this is not to be wasted then the problems of present day pollution will need to be tackled.

For the city, as a World Heritage Site, it is surprising how much attention is placed on the buildings and how little is paid to their surroundings. This has been taken to the extreme recently with the erection of concrete bollards on Pulteney Bridge in conjunction with excessive road signing. Many pavements have been torn up and replaced with precast concrete slabs or more recently, concrete block paving. These materials have their place, but surely not within the conservation area. A programme to replace the railings in some of the more notable locations should be undertaken. This has already been accomplished in St James's Square as well as Catharine Place and is at last happening gradually in Victoria Park. Some of the roads still have pennant setts left in position beneath the macadam. Maybe some of these could be brought to light again.

I will close with some notes relating the more significant publishers of pictures in this book. The letters in brackets following the title refer to the relevant publisher mentioned below.

Dawson & Dutton (D&D) have provided many of the early views in this publication. They were situated at 44 Milsom Street from 1862. The following year Dawson left the firm and the brothers John and James Dutton (DU) continued on their own until 1867, before moving to 21 Bathwick Street. In 1872, they moved again, this time to 6 Henrietta Villas and traded under the name of Dutton Brothers until 1877. Finally after another move to 4 Prince's Buildings, the studio finally closed in 1891.

A George Dafnis appears in the Bath Post Office Directory as a lodging house keeper at 8 Pulteney Street in 1874. Moving in 1900 to 40 Pulteney Street he is last recorded in 1917. Yet it is most likely to be his son George Love Dafnis (DA) who was the photographer responsible for the views shown here. They seem to have been taken largely during two periods, the first from around 1908 to 1915 and the second during the 1930s. He lived at 32 Sydney Buildings from 1911 until his death in 1968.

Charles Edward Viner (V) was a baker and confectioner, at 17 Kingsmead Square and 41 Livingstone Road from 1916–35, later becoming C.E. Viner Ltd. and closing about 1955. He also ran the Post Office at George's House, George's Place, Bathwick Hill (1916–18). It is during this period that I believe he was responsible for producing an enormous quantity of photographic post cards, from North Somerset and South Wales. Previously he must have operated from Weston Super Mare as this is the address printed on the earliest cards, but by 1915 he had moved to Bath, living at Taringa, Bloomfield Park. At a later date, the York Publishing Co. of Bristol took over his business.

Francis Jones (J) was a newsagent and tobacconist at 15 Margaret Buildings, starting in business in 1894. Two years later he is recorded as a stationer and bookseller and eventually acquired number fourteen as well. He ran the business until 1938, but most of the photographs were taken around 1905.

Frank George Goodall (GO), began his career as a printer at 1 St Mary's Buildings in 1890. The firm became Goodall & Sons, now printers and stationers at 18 & 19 Westgate Street in 1898. Frank Goodall had given up the business by 1905 to become a traveller and was finally recorded as a resident in 1907. The firm continued to go from strength to strength and later amalgamated with W. & F. Dawson.

Henry Long (L) was largely a portrait photographer, but he also photographed street scenes as well as private homes. He had several addresses, firstly at 6 Canterbury Road (1904–7), then 11 Triangle Villas (1908–9). In 1910 he moved to Combe Down at 2 Pleasant View, then in 1912 to 94 Entry Hill where he remained until 1938.

Other publishers of note are Francis Frith & Co. Ltd of Reigate (F), Carpenter of Ramsgate (C), Garratt of Bristol (GA), R. Wilkinson & Co. of Trowbridge (W) and Lucien Levy (LL), printed under licence from the Levy family of Paris.

Finally, I hope you find as much enjoyment studying this book as I have had in compiling it.

One
Southgate to Northgate

OLD BRIDGE (C) 1905. Originally called St Lawrence's Bridge and erected in 1362, it was rebuilt in 1754. In August 1823 plans were drawn up by Thomas Telford for a replacement bridge. James Dredge later also had a scheme, but it was widened instead. The bridge was removed as part of a road improvement scheme in 1964. In the background are the chimneys of the Bath Corporation Electric Lighting Works of 1890.

SOUTHGATE STREET (V) *c.* 1915. Previously called Horse Street, it was widened in 1805 when the western side was rebuilt and was followed by the eastern side in 1826. Nothing in this view survives today as the left side was rebuilt in 1965 and the other in 1971. The Full Moon Hotel was owned by Alfred J. Tanner (1890–1921), but was pulled down in 1931 to make way for the electricity headquarters. Opposite was Eastman's Ltd (1890–1926), one of a chain of butchers' shops.

SOUTHGATE STREET (GO) OCT 1882. Here we can see a view of the street during one of the many severe floods that took place up until 1968. The Full Moon at this time was occupied by Alfred R. Tanner (1866–89). On the corner of Dorchester Street was William Bright, a pharmaceutical chemist (*c.* 1846–83). On the left side were the businesses of Frederick Hawkins, a grocer (1874–1908) and John Davis who was a house decorator (1880–8).

ARGYLE TEMPERENCE HOTEL, MANVERS STREET *c.* 1915. This was run by J.W. Mitchell, cook and confectioner, between 1904 and 1920. The left side of the hotel forms a part of Railway Place. It started life in about 1844 as the Commercial Coffee House and Family Hotel, later known as the Great Western Commercial Hotel. Now black and shabby, it closed as the Argyle Private and Commercial Hotel in about 1957. W.H. Smith & Sons newsagency was here from 1908–26 and there is still a shop trading here today.

FURZE'S RESTAURANT, RAILWAY PLACE *c.* 1930. This property was destroyed in the blitz and has never been replaced. It is now an unsightly open space by the exit of the bus station that was once Railway Road. Bramwell Kemiston Furze owned the premises from 1910 until its destruction and was also the owner of a hotel in Southgate Street.

SOUTHGATE STREET (W) 1908. The buildings that replaced these are a prime example of bad planning. When the shops close, everything dies. What has become of the residents and the night life? On the left was William Holloway's butcher's store (1894–1971), with Hodder's the chemists (1906–69) next door. On the right were Boots Cash Chemists and Alfred Dodge, a grocer. The Noah's Ark sign belonged to Cramond & Sons, stationers. The two public houses, the Golden Lion Hotel and the New Inn closed in 1923 and 1961 respectively.

LOWER BOROUGH WALLS AND ST. JAMES'S CHURCH c. 1925. The church was designed by John Palmer in 1768. Altered in 1848, it was blitzed in 1942 and demolished in 1957. On the left Percy Edward's cycle shop has lost its pitched roof and is now Lloyd's Bank. Next door O. Newman & Son's building was replaced in 1928. On the right was the North West London Meat Co. shop (1919–70) followed by William Dawson & Sons, newsagents. This and all beyond it have been blitzed or redeveloped.

STALL ST. BATH. 31.

STALL STREET (GA) 1915. This superb post card shows a part of the city that has changed dramatically. The corner of Southgate Street just appears on the left with Boots Cash Chemists. Proceeding along the left side of Stall Street is Olinthus Newman's ironmongery and china store, then Cecil Stuckey, a gentleman's outfitter (1908–15). On the right side was Lennards Ltd, boot warehouse (opened in 1914), followed by Charles Grant, a greengrocer, florist and fruiterer (1909–34). The second block beyond Abbeygate Street on the right, was pulled down in 1933.

SOUTH PARADE *c.* 1880. On the left today are George's and Pratt's Hotels, which were then private houses, built by John Wood in 1743. One or two of the roadside trees remain. St John the Evangelist Church, built by Charles Hanson, was started on 29 September 1861, consecrated on 5 October 1864 and has survived despite bomb damage in 1942. Sadly the gardens on the right have long gone and are now occupied by a car park and the Police Station.

NORTH PARADE BRIDGE (F) 1876. Built by William Clark, it was opened on 10 November 1836. When encased in Bath stone in 1936, the toll houses were replaced by small stairways. The Mason's Arms in Ferry Place can be seen through the arch of the bridge. The river bank is now much neater, with its paving and boat moorings.

THE PAVILION (DA) *c.* 1935. Now much cleaner, but not the amenity that many people of Bath wish for. At this time it stood alone, but is now surrounded by a car park and the sports centre. Needless to say the illuminated signpost has long gone.

NORTH PARADE AND TERRACE WALKS (DU) *c*. 1868. On the corner of Pierrepont Street was William Everitt, a print seller and artists' colourman. Starting in business at Pulteney Bridge in about 1837, he also had this shop between 1868 and 1879. The two houses in Pierrepont Street on the left have since become shops. North Parade was begun in 1740 by John Wood, but these houses weren't converted into a hotel until 1879 when the Fernley House Hotel opened. What happened to the statue of Queen Elizabeth located between the windows which had disappeared before the turn of the century? The building behind the right hand Bath Chair, dating from about 1750, belonged to Francis Danger (1860–9) a wine merchant on Terrace Walks. Now the Huntsman public house, it has since had major changes made to the shop front.

17

ROYAL LITERARY AND SCIENTIFIC INSTITUTION (DU) *c.* 1865. This important building was shamefully pulled down for road a improvement as long ago as 1933. On the left is the Ale House public house, which was then a wine and spirit vaults occupied by Mrs Anne Vezey (*c.* 1856–67). All the houses visible in York Street have today been converted into shops.

ROYAL LITERARY AND SCIENTIFIC INSTITUTION *c.* 1930. Initially named the Lower Rooms, built in 1806, they were rebuilt following a serious fire on 21 December 1820. Upon reopening in 1825, they incorporated part of the south side and portico of the earlier building. There were once reading rooms, libraries, museums of geology, antiquities and natural history housed here. The old library premises in Queen Square have recently become their replacement. This view is from the rear, with Orange Grove on the right.

PARADE GARDENS (DA) *c.* 1935. This view results from the demolition of the Royal Literary and Scientific Institution and is very much how it looks today. The gardens, renamed on reopening, are still very popular and immaculately kept. The Edward VII memorial by the steps was moved here from George Street in July 1933.

BATH ABBEY FROM ORANGE GROVE *c.* 1880. Slightly later than the following picture, the Abbey Hotel is now in the hands of Caleb Davis (1878–83) and has gained an unsightly metal chimney. Note the cab stand near Rebecca Fountain and also the royal coat of arms on Jacob Smith's (1876–81) butcher's shop in Cheap Street.

BATH ABBEY FROM ORANGE GROVE (DU) *c.* 1866. The Abbey replaces a Norman structure and was started in 1499, but had to be restored following a visit to Bath by Queen Elizabeth in 1574. It can be seen before the new pinnacles were constructed in 1906. All the buildings on the far right were demolished long ago, to be replaced by the extension to the Guildhall. The obelisk in Orange Grove was erected in 1734. James Downton had the Abbey Hotel from 1866 to 1871. The White Hart Hotel, which was removed in 1867 can be seen through the Abbey Church Yard. At the end of Cheap Street was Alfred Willison's chemist shop (1860–9), now the London Camera Exchange.

ABBEY CHURCH YARD (F) 1876. James Davies' shop was pulled down in 1892 for John Brydon's Concert Hall and beside this is the Pump Room. The Colonnade designed by Thomas Baldwin in 1786 is dwarfed by the Grand Pump Room Hotel which opened in June 1869. Requisitioned during the war, it never reopened and was demolished in 1959.

THE GUILDHALL *c.* 1890. The first was built by Inigo Jones in 1625. The present building was started in 1766, but construction was interrupted until 1775 when new designs were submitted by Thomas Baldwin. It was finally completed in 1777. Looking from an upper floor of a building opposite, this shows it before the new wings were added by John Brydon between 1893 and 1895.

HIGH STREET (GA) 1915. Here we can see the Guildhall following the addition of the new wings. The public telephone in the foreground was a fairly recent addition to the street scene, but has since gone.

W. & F. DAWSON, HIGH STREET c. 1906. These premises were used as a printers, stationers and account book manufacturers. Established in 1770, Dawson took over the business from Charles Hunt in about 1852. In 1935, on merging as Dawson & Goodall, they moved elsewhere. The building went in 1969 and is now an unattractive office block occupied by the Woolwich Building Society. To its left is part of the Christopher Hotel which now has a rebuilt facade of dubious appearance.

HIGH STREET (GO) 1904. As mentioned above, the Goddard's shop has gone as has The Union of London & Smiths Bank Ltd. (1904–18). Established in 1760 this has been tastefully rebuilt. Named the Old Bank, it is still used for that purpose. Cooper & Sons Ltd, a boot warehouse, is now JCR News. Next to this is the Corridor which has a large glass canopy added. The buildings beyond are still standing and J.W. Crook & Sons, tailors, hatters, hosiers and outfitters have been there since 1908.

J.R. GODDARD, HIGH STREET (GO) 1904. What a delight it must have been to walk into a shop and see a display like this. John Goddard was a fruit salesman and commission agent between 1902 and 1939. The facade of his shop was painted with great skill and is very attractive. This practise for some reason appears to be taboo today, yet many businesses must have advertised in this way from when they were were built.

THE CORRIDOR *c.* 1905. This arcade was designed by Henry Goodridge. It opened in 1825 and the glass roof was added in 1870. This view was taken looking away from the High Street. The paving has changed and the gates at each end went recently. A major renovation followed the IRA bomb in the early 1970s.

HIGH STREET (LL) 1905. A scene of activity, but not nearly as busy as a Saturday in the 1990s. On the left is the Guildhall with the new wing, housing the Bath Technical School. George Oliver's boot and shoe warehouse (1884–*c.*1940) is on the right with the glorious hanging lamps. This and the adjoining buildings belonging to Cater, Stoffell & Fortt Ltd (1890–1985) were taken down in about 1964 and replaced by a new block that should never have got any further than the drawing board.

78 BATH. — Northgate Street. - LL.

NORTHGATE STREET (LL) 1905. Widened when the North Gate was demolished in 1755, the houses date from 1805 to 1810. Designed by G.P. Manvers on the site of previous churches, the foundation stone of St. Michael's Church was laid on 21 April 1835. Having recently been superbly cleaned, only the railings need renewing. On the right, Fisher & Co. (1878–1916) were cooks, confectioners, restaurateurs and wine merchants. Only the first two houses in this rank now survive, the others having been cut down to make way for the appalling Hilton Hotel and also the Podium. On the corner of New Bond Street were the premises of John Rubie, wine merchant and owner of the Castle Hotel (1860–1906). Again, all have now gone to make way for the Post Office which opened in 1928.

Two

Queen Square to
Queen Square Station

COUNTY CLUB, QUEEN SQUARE (C) 1905. The square was named after Queen Caroline and built by John Wood between 1728 and 1736. The club is still in existence, but the Virginia creeper has now spread even further across the building. The post box has gone, along with the lamp column, but apart from traffic furniture there has been little change.

75 BATH. — *Prince's Street.* — LL.

EDGAR BUILDINGS (LL) 1905. Dating from 1762, a grand porch now adorns the newly restored P.J. Pepper's cafe-bar. Beyond Bartlett Street are Prince's Buildings, originally to be called Princess Buildings after Princess Amelia. Opposite are York Buildings and the York House Hotel, all built by John Wood from 1759.

MILSOM STREET (GA) 1915. Started in 1762, this was once a residential street. The car (Y 3285) was a 25hp Fiat Limousine Landaulette. The National Westminster Bank on the left is now the Bath Environmental Centre.

OLD BOND STREET AND BURTON STREET (DA) *c.* 1935. Taken on a miserable day, these must have been the earliest set of traffic lights in Bath. Old Bond Street was built in 1769, but only half of the central block remains, the rest having been removed in 1872. At the front is E.P. Mallory & Sons Ltd, gold and silversmiths, still here today. On the right is the Bernina Swiss Cafe and Theobald's cafe, lately Carwardine's coffee house. On the left is Burton Street, erected in 1781.

NEW BOND STREET 1904. Building of this street started in 1805. Henry Gillard & Co's (1888–1963), tea and coffee shop is actually in New Bond Street Place. Until recently this was Bilbo's book shop. Next door is Frank Batchelor's mantle warehouse with Henry Hodder & Co. Ltd., the chemists, opposite (1904–69). The far right has now been rebuilt by leaving the facades intact and at the end now stands the grandiose Podium. Unfortunately the canopies to keep the rain off are little used these days.

QUEEN STREET AND TRIM BRIDGE *c.* 1930. This was one of the first streets to have been built outside the city walls in 1707. St John's Gatehouse passes over it and has recently been cleaned, losing the street nameplate on the right. Elsie Shellard's shop can be seen and is a part of the Canary Cafe today. Opposite in Trim Street is R.J. Bossi, watch and clockmaker (1924–68), now the Trim Street Gallery. In the distance is Bridewell Lane and part of the Blue Coat Charity School.

UNION STREET 1904. Proposed in 1789 and finished by Thomas Baldwin in 1806, it has now been pedestrianized. This is the junction of Stall Street, Westgate Street and Cheap Street. On the left was Stephen Fox-Andrews, established 1868 and at present is Clark's shoe shop. On the right, demolished in the 1930s, was J. Hepworth & Son Ltd., clothiers (1895–1911), followed by A.H. Foster, fancy draper, hosier, hatter, shirtmaker and tailor (1903–4). This corner has recently been taken by Dixon's stores.

UNION PASSAGE (W) 1906. A rebuilding of Cock Lane, the earliest lease dates from 1789. On the right, built in brick, were the Military Arms (1870–1906), Leonard Caddell, a hairdresser (1906–10), and William Hart, newsagent (1858–1913). This alleyway appears so dull today when compared to the view seen here.

ROYAL UNITED HOSPITAL, HOT BATH STREET (F) 1901. Hot Bath Street dates from 1805 and has been repaved with uncharacteristic granite setts. On the right was the Hetling Pump House and the on the corner, since rebuilt, were the premises of John Sculthorpe, tailor, draper, etc. (1858–1904). The United Hospital was founded in 1824 and opened on 24 June 1826. The Albert wing replaced the Bath City Infirmary and Dispensary in 1864. Both are at last getting a long deserved facelift.

CHAPEL COURT c. 1910. Built in about 1770, this view is from Westgate Buildings. Some of the buildings were demolished in 1967 to make way for the Master's Lodge of the Hospital of St John the Baptist. This included the central building (No. 6) which has been replaced in a similar style, but the houses to the left, occupied by the Monmouth Street Society remain and amazingly so do the railings.

ROSEWELL HOUSE, KINGSMEAD SQUARE (DA) *c*. 1915. Built in 1736 by Strahan, the shop front had not long been altered. George Sheppard's stores are now used as a newsagents. The Midland Dairy in New Street was built in about 1870 following the removal of earlier buildings along this side of the square. On the corner of Kingsmead Street is William Crook, a fish and fruit salesman (1910–5), followed by the Star Temperance Hotel and refreshment rooms (1896–1932).

WOTTON BROTHERS, MILK STREET *c*. 1930. Starting as steam haulage contractors in 1917, by 1923 they had become quarry owners. In 1929 they became a limited company and remained in Milk Street until 1934, when they opened offices at 17 George Street. In 1967 these were closed and operations were transferred to the quarry at Wick. The yard has now gone, along with most of the street. Registered in Bath, this diesel powered Mercedes Benz L6500 was a very rare vehicle to these shores.

MIDLAND RAILWAY HOTEL,
JAMES STREET WEST *c.* 1906.
Opened in 1868 it did not stand alone,
as the house next door has been blanked
out in the picture. William Freeman was
only here for three years (1906–8). The
name was shortened to the Midland
Hotel in 1915 and it has since been
rebuilt. Previously James Street, the
West was added in 1892. This is
possibly Bath's most oppressive area.

GREEN PARK STATION,
SEYMOUR STREET *c.* 1914. Built on
the west side of the street, houses from
1792–5 were demolished to make way
for the station. Initially called Queen
Square Station, the first trains arrived
on Wednesday 4 August 1869. To the
left of the canopy is now the entrance
to Sainsbury's food store and the Green
Park Brasserie occupies the booking
hall. Although restored to its former
glory, the lamp and paved area have
long since disappeared.

MIDLAND STATION, BATH.

Three
Pulteney Bridge to The Paragon

PULTENEY BRIDGE (W) *c.* 1905. This elegant design by Robert Adam was built between 1769 and 1774. The southwest end had been shortened in 1908, but it has since been restored to the original design. This restoration has also resulted in a uniformity of shop fronts. Laying pennant setts in the road and restricting the flow of traffic would be an excellent method of completing the restoration.

PULTENEY BRIDGE AND WEIR (DU) *c.* 1865. This is now a very different scene indeed. All that remains today is the bridge, Newmarket Row to the left, Bridge Street in the background and the end of Argyle Buildings on the right. The rear of Orange Grove can be seen at the left of the picture. Between this and the River Avon were the Town Mills, which were all removed in the 1890s in readiness for construction of the Empire Hotel. The timber market building adjoining Pulteney Bridge is no longer with us, nor is the weir. This has been very successfully redesigned, apart from the sluice gate and the silted boat mooring. Also taken down is the Bathwick flour and cloth mill on the right. All of this area alongside the river has been tidied up to form a pleasant riverside walk.

PULTENEY BRIDGE (F) 1901. This is a very different looking bridge from that today. A few years later improvements were made by removing the extensions and the chimney. Madame Jane Hamilton was a corset and belt maker and William Roworth a watchmaker. A path to the river replaces the single storey structure on the right.

LAURA PLACE (GA) 1915. This tree-lined square was named after Henrietta Laura Pulteney. The fountain was changed considerably and all the decorative chains and shrubs have gone. On the right in Argyle Street is Argyle Chapel, opened in 1790.

PULTENEY STREET (DU) *c.* 1865. Built in 1789 from plans by Thomas Baldwin, here we see the street before any trees were planted. The houses on the left became a part of the Pulteney Hotel, established in 1866, soon after this picture was taken. It has now closed and been converted into flats. There is no fountain in Laura Place to celebrate the centenary of the Royal Bath and West Show as it was not unveiled until 14 July 1880. At the end is the Bath Proprietory College, originally the Sydney Hotel.

SAINSBURY BROTHERS, LAURA PLACE *c.* 1935. This shows one of their delivery lorries at work. The firm has been operating under variations of the Sainsbury name for over two centuries. They have occupied 3 Edgar Buildings since 1839 and also had the London Brewery at the end of Nelson Terrace until it closed in 1901.

PULTENEY ROAD (C) 1905. This street laid out by Harcourt Masters was to have been called Sackville Street. Taken from the junction with North Parade Road, the end of the old convent can just be seen. Beside it was Lorne Villas, now St John's Junior School, it has a very large extension added to the left of the chimney stack and the front wall has gone. Some of these trees are still growing, some have been replaced, but they will never look like this again.

SYDNEY BUILDINGS c. 1910. Built between 1821 and 1832, this is a view of the rear of Sydney Parade, a part of Sydney Buildings, and was taken from Rasamar Lock. The buildings still look very similar, but many have now been painted. Today the canal bank is no longer cultivated or as well covered by trees.

HORSESHOE WALK (C) 1905. This view is directed towards Widcombe, beyond Sydney Buildings. It is quite different these days, with detached 1920s houses on the right, but is still tree lined and rural on the left hand side of the road.

THE KENNET AND AVON CANAL (L) *c.* 1920. This photograph was taken from the top lock of the canal. The malthouse on the right in Sydney Buildings has become the offices of David Kent architects. Bathwick Hill passes over the canal bridge in the distance. The houses on the far left are the rear of George's Place. Between these and the bridge were George's House and some canalside cottages. They have all been replaced by a Mercedes Benz car showroom and the site screened by trees.

VIEW FROM BATHWICK TERRACE, APRIL 1874. The terrace was built in 1842, soon after the railway and is situated below George's Place. In the distance can be seen the fresh stonework of the Convent de la Sainte Union des Sacres Coeurs (1861) and St John's Roman Catholic Church just enters the picture on the right. The two houses by the railway are Pulteney House and Grove Lodge.

ST MARY'S CHURCH (DU) c. 1865. Replacing an earlier church, the first stone was laid on 1 September 1814 and it was consecrated on 4 February 1820. Sadly it is now far from clean. Both this and Raby Place on the right were built by John Pinch the elder. The house now has no canopy over the door, the windows have glazing bars and the tree alongside has grown to maturity since. Darlington Street can be seen in the background. Traffic and associated paraphernalia clutter this scene today.

DARLINGTON STREET (L) *c.* 1925. The first leases were issued in 1791, although it was not built until 1810. The archway leads to the premises of Herbert Woodman. He started working here as a chauffeur in 1920, but ended up a garage owner until it's closure in 1929. Little has changed in this view. The buildings to the right of the archway have been cleaned, the advertisement and lamp are no more. As one of the main routes through Bath, it has now become very congested.

BATH PROPRIETORY COLLEGE, SYDNEY GARDENS *c.* 1865. The first stone of this house, designed by Charles Harcourt Masters, was laid on 15 November 1796. Built as the Sydney Hotel, it became a college in about 1855. Now the Holburne Museum, it had substantial alterations made between 1913 and 1916. The walls on either side have been replaced by colonnades, the windows beneath the portico have gone and the parapet is very ornate with decorative urns on the corners.

SYDNEY GARDENS (V) *c.* 1915. A very pleasant place to go to get away from the hustle and bustle of life. It was laid out by Harcourt Masters in 1795. This picture was taken from the entrance in Bathwick Street. Very little has changed in this view except that the sign has gone and there are now two buildings similar to this. The one here is hidden behind laurel bushes these days.

FORESTER ROAD (C) 1905. Construction of this street started in 1898. Viewed from the junction with Warminster Road, all appears much the same today. After the large trees on the left is Powlett Road and on the right is a house called Yatesbury.

POWLETT ROAD (C) 1905. This view is facing towards Fairfield Park and appears as in the post card to this very day. These houses were built in 1894 and unusually for this part of the world they were constructed mainly of brick.

BATH HYDRO, OFF SYDNEY ROAD c. 1913. This was a once a large mansion called Vellore, built about 1835 and became the Bath College between 1877 and 1909. From 1915 it was The Bath Spa Hotel and later a nurses' home, but has now returned to being a hotel. The central building is still just as grand, but the two-storey addition to its right has been replaced by a well-built five-storey block. The taxi was a Sharron goods van which belonged to Bristol Tramways and Carriage Co. Ltd.

THE KENNET AND AVON CANAL (C) 1905. This is the swing bridge looking towards the city and is still in good working order. It is situated just above what was Cremorne Gardens and the Grosvenor Brewery, which were hit by a stray bomb during the Bath blitz.

BATHWICK STREET (L) c. 1920. Built between 1792 and 1795, occupying the site of the village, of which by 1790 only the Crown Inn existed. The van (FB 1536) belonged to Bath Tramways Parcel Service. Albert Avery, dairyman and grocer (1917–24), had the shop on the left with John Harding, a grocer, alongside (1890–1937). The Crown public house is the third on this site and lost its ivy when recently cleaned. The Jet petrol filling station has yet to arrive beyond the houses on the left.

BATHWICK STREET (LL) *c.* 1905. This view was taken from outside the modern and less than fitting Henrietta Court, with Rochfort Place behind the photographer. Apart from the constant queues of traffic, only the loss of some of the trees to make way for the fire and ambulance stations have changed this scene.

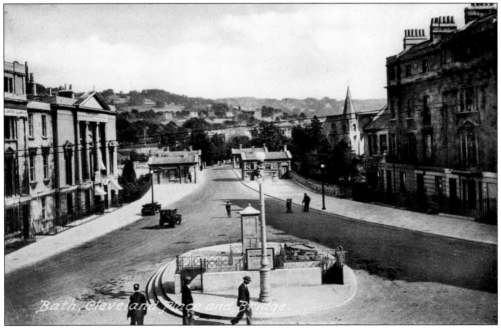

CLEVELAND PLACE (F) 1929. The right side was constructed by Henry Goodridge in 1828, apart from the curious little Victorian house of 1869. When the other side was completed it became known as Cleveland Place East and West. Nearest the bridge is the Eastern Dispensary which opened in 1845. The traffic island still exists, but has expanded into a large triangular affair. The bridge was also by Goodridge and opened on 28 September 1827. In the background is St John the Baptist Church.

CLEVELAND PLACE EAST (W) *c.* 1923. Taken from Walcot Parade, the end house by the steps is a part of Anglo Terrace built for the workers of the Walcot Brewery behind. On the corner was Herbert Broad, a chemist (1915–28), now the Dixy Fried Chicken take-away. The Bath & West of England College of Chemistry and Pharmacy (1908–29) has become HRS Motorcycle Shop and the house to it's right the Bath Charcoal Grill. These two premises have had large plate glass shop windows installed. Note the monument on the traffic island.

LONDON STREET 1865. The first houses were built around 1770. Somerset Buildings on the right became unsafe due to the Hedgemead landslip and were taken down in about 1880. Hedgemead Park was created to replace them, opening on 1 July 1889. In the centre is St Swithun's church, built by John Palmer in 1780 and today beautifully restored, except for the railings which are on their last legs. Just visible on the left is the Hat and Feather public house, but not the present one which dates from 1900.

GUINEA LANE (V) c. 1915. This is Hedgemead Park on the left following the removal of Somerset Buildings. Large trees in the park now obscure this view. The large building on the right was St Swithun's National School of 1840. Now an antiques market, this must be one of the dirtiest buildings in Bath. On the corner was the Somerset Dairy, run by Walter North (1904–18) and beyond is Axford Buildings and St Swithun's church.

AXFORD BUILDINGS c. 1906. Taken from the corner of Vineyards and Guinea Lane, these houses were built by Thomas Atwood in 1769 and named after John Axford, at one time a Mayor of Bath. At the residents' request they were combined with Paragon Buildings in 1866 and the whole was renamed the Paragon. All the window awnings have gone and the post box is a modern replacement, otherwise little has changed.

PARAGON BUILDINGS AND HAY HILL (F) 1911. On the left are Fountain Buildings and Hay Hill Baptist Chapel. Taking about a year to build, it opened on 4 May 1870. The shop on the right occupied by Henry Wood, bookseller, stationer and librarian (1903–39) at Bladud's Buildings is now occupied by the Hub, a night club and live music venue. Beyond this are Paragon Buildings, built in 1769, again by Thomas Atwood. Note how decorative the street lamp is compared to present day examples.

FOUNTAIN BUILDINGS (W) c. 1908. Erected by John Wood the Younger in 1770, the cycle shop on the corner has been restored and is now the Fountain Antiques Centre. What happened to the fountain in front of the shop, put up in 1860 by the Bath Licensed Victuallers and the RSPCA, to replace an earlier one? Most of the stores on the hill have been recently converted for housing. On the left was the end of Prince's Buildings, later rebuilt with a curved facade and on the right Bladud's Buildings dating from 1755.

Four
Lansdown to Lambridge

OXFORD ROW AND BELMONT (C) 1905. This view has been taken from the end of Alfred Street. Oxford Row, built about 1780, is on the left with Bennett Street beyond. Belmont, on the right, was built by John Wood the Younger in 1770. Other than many of the houses having been cleaned, little has changed.

BATH EYE INFIRMARY, BELVEDERE *c.* 1911. This row of buildings was erected in 1775 and was originally called Lansdown Street. The Infirmary opened in 1811 in Bath Street, but for twenty seven years from 1862 it occupied the house on the right. From 1907, it expanded to occupy both properties and remained here until 1973, when they were converted into flats. Apart from an external clean and new windows with glazing bars, the building is as seen in the picture.

RIVERS STREET AND RUSSEL STREET *c.* 1906. Rivers Street was built between 1775 and 1786 and named after Sir Peter Rivers. Just visible is the canopy of the Montpelier Bakery. Behind is Christ Church, dating from 1795. Russel Street, by John Wood the Younger (1775), was named after an apothecary who had a botanical garden here. The wooden street sign has now gone, thus revealing it's proper spelling with just one l. The end house was changed by the removal of the single storey entrance hall.

RUSSEL STREET (J) 1904. This view is looking up from Bennett Street. The houses on the right still have their shutters and are just as soot blackened today. Further along the left side of the street today is the Queensberry Hotel. At the top in Rivers Street was the Montpelier Bakery, run by Miss B.C. Robbins between 1901 and 1917 and in the windows can be seen advertisements for Cadbury's chocolate. This is now a clothing shop called Gear Change.

BENNETT STREET (J) 1904. The buildings date from 1764, but the Francis' Private Hotel wasn't established until 1883. By the time its fate had been sealed in the blitz it was known as the Regina Hotel. Now rebuilt from Doulting stone, it is yet another of the city's hotels to have closed as it has been turned into flats. Although it looks similar, the lack of any doors along the facade creates an odd appearance. On the left where the additional doorway once stood is Circus Place.

THE CIRCUS *c.* 1910. Designed by John Wood, construction started in 1754, but by 1762 was only two thirds complete. A decision was made recently to extract the railing bases and keep the centre an open space, with the large plane trees in the middle. The taxi waiting for a fare was a Sharron Hackney. In Bennett Street the two shops were destroyed in the war. They belonged to George Davie, baker and confectioner (1909–14), and Sidney Foster, dyer and cleaner (1907–17), and were replaced by a house quite out of keeping with the surroundings.

GAY STREET (V) *c.* 1915. This street was designed by John Wood and completed by Wood the Younger in 1762. The picture was taken from the corner of George Street and still looks much the same today, apart from the cleanliness of the houses.

BROCK STREET (J) 1904. Built between 1765 and 1766 by John Wood the Younger, this elegant street linked the Royal Crescent and the Circus. On the right where Cobb Farr, the estate agents now trade was one of several outlets belonging to the Bath & Somersetshire Dairy Co. Ltd. (1886–1920). This has since lost its canopy. The Circus Restaurant nearby had a similar front, but it had gone by this time. The ornate street light on the left still stands, although no longer gas lit.

MARGARET'S BUILDINGS (J) 1904. Built by Wood the Younger, they were badly damaged during the war. Looking from Brock Street, on the right, the grocers, now awaiting a new owner, has sadly lost its decorative shop front. The shop front of Victor Blyth, general contractor and house decorator (1897–1937), was later copied onto a post war building. On the left was Mrs L. Rudman, milliner and fancy draper (1898–1905). The building beyond the single-storey shops has lost its upper floors today.

ROYAL CRESCENT *c.* 1948. Another project by John Wood the younger, the first stone was laid on 17 May 1767, the work taking until 1775 to complete. Outside number nineteen are two newly acquired delivery vans belonging to Cyril Howe the photographer and camera shop owner. AFB 634 is a Jowett Bradford van and GL 9618 is an Austin.

MARLBOROUGH BUILDINGS (V) *c.* 1915. This is seen from the bottom of the row and shows just how to construct a terrace on a hillside. Built between 1789 and 1791, today the covered balcony has been taken away from the second house and all the window shutters and awnings have gone. On the opposite side a narrow footway has been squeezed alongside the railings and the big tree in the distance has been felled.

MARLBOROUGH BUILDINGS (V) *c.* 1915. Opening as the Marlborough Tavern, it was built at about the same time as the main rank of houses. Later renamed the Marlborough Hotel, Arthur Candy was the licensee at this time. It returned to its first name in about 1966. The painted sign, once so familiar on the walls of many business premises, especially public houses, has since been partly replaced by an extra window.

CAVENDISH PLACE (C) 1905. Started in 1808 by John Pinch the elder and completed in 1815, these buildings are unusual for this city in that the ground floor facades are painted. For some reason all the canopies have been removed, yet the balconies remain. The residents are fortunate in having delightful views of Victoria Park from here. The wall on the left belongs to Cavendish Villa, seen in the view over the page.

CAVENDISH VILLA 1906. Set just above Cavendish Place this lovely little detached house appears to have been constructed in about 1852. With its long, well-kept garden, and set well back from the road, it remains very similar today, although it has lost its veranda and only the end chimney stack survives.

PARK STREET (V) c. 1915. Situated at the north west corner of St James's Square, it was built between 1791 and 1793. The street was never quite completed at the top end and for a long time a partially built single storey facade could be seen on the right side. Building work has been carried out recently to make it into a habitable dwelling. Another house has just been completed on the left side of the road.

58

GREAT BEDFORD STREET *c.* 1906. Built at about the same time as Park Street, we have now moved to the north east side of St James's Square. The first two houses on the east side of the street are still standing, but following the blitz the remainder were replaced by an uninspiring block of flats.

LANSDOWN ROAD *c.* 1955. These houses were numbers 18, 19, and 20 from right to left. Demolished by 1968, all that remains today are part of the facades to window level. These should be rebuilt to hide the horrors behind. The pillar, in what was Mount Pleasant, is nothing more than a footpath now. To the right, replacing homes taken down soon after 1903, was the road leading to Lampard's Buildings.

ST ANDREW'S CHURCH *c.* 1880. Harley House was pulled down in 1859 in readiness for erecting the church. Built between 1870 and 1873, the 240 feet tall tower was added in 1879. Now an open space, behind the church was a row of shops called Abingdon Buildings, also blitzed. Through the tree, Upper Church Street ended at Rivers Street, so in about 1890, to connect it with Julian Road, Harley Place was removed.

BELVEDERE HOUSE, BELVEDERE c. 1930. This shop hasn't changed much, even the short length of railings still survives. Now occupied by Feature Fireplaces, Clement James Weetman was a greengrocer and fruiterer from 1929 until 1987. The path to the right leads to Wellington Place and Wellington Terrace, once called Ford's Place.

CITY VIEW *c*. 1930. In Camden Road, near to Camden Crescent, this block of houses was built in 1871. On the extreme left is the end of Berkeley Place shown in the picture below and now painted white. The façade has changed little, apart from some stone cleaning. The street lamp on the corner of the crescent is no longer to be seen.

BERKELEY PLACE *c*. 1930. Constructed in 1873, it is still very much as seen here. The footway and the retaining wall holding back the gardens of Upper Camden place have since been rebuilt.

SOMERSET PLACE (V) *c.* 1915. Dating from 1793, it should have been named Spackman's Buildings. Although the creeper has gone, a large tree has up grown outside the front of number fifteen. The last three houses on the end were all refaced after the bombing. Today many of the houses are used by the Bath College of Higher Education.

LANSDOWN CRESCENT (F) 1876. Designed by John Palmer and built between 1789 and 1793, this view is from Lansdown Place East. The awnings on the first house have gone as has the intaglio street name, frequently to be seen painted in this style at this time.

RICHMOND PLACE c. 1910. These houses seen here are set along the side of Beacon Hill Common. On the right the post office was the one next to the tree, located here from 1906 until 1910. It moved three times during its lifetime, having opened in 1895 and lasting until 1915. The wider entrance on the right led to the Rising Sun public house and grocer's shop, which closed in 1937. When first opened in 1872 it was named the Sun Inn.

CLAREMONT TERRACE c. 1908. At the end of Camden Road, this terrace was built in about 1846. On the corner is Frankley House and the shop next door, called Camden House, was occupied by Mrs Ethel Page, a draper (1906–38). The dairy established in 1885 has closed and the shop fronts have been extended since this picture was taken. By this time the Rising Sun has already had a much larger extension added. The other buildings beyond it, on the corner of Tyning Lane, were taken down a few years ago.

LONDON ROAD (V) *c.* 1915. The newsagent's by Upper East Hayes on the right, now a house, belonged to Charles Morris. This is Kensington Cottages, Mile End. Kensington Place is on the left and unlike below, it now has trees planted along the front.

KENSINGTON PLACE (DU) *c.* 1865. Kensington Chapel opened on 4 January 1790, it closed in 1930 and is badly in need of a facelift. This early picture was taken before any trees were planted and when the road was at a lower level. The prominent house on the left is Kensington House, dating from 1793.

OTAGO TERRACE, LARKHALL *c.* 1909. This is a terrace of 35 houses started in 1886. Cottage Place and Budbrook Place on the right all went in the 1960s to be replaced by awful reconstructed stone houses. Catsley Place is beyond, now half missing.

LONDON ROAD, LAMBRIDGE *c.* 1911. Taken from the bottom of the Gloucester Road, there are few changes here, apart from an appalling block of flats in the garden of Montague House on the right. Alfred Walters took over the Kensington Nursery in 1874. Oxford Gardens, seen here, opened in 1911 and is still trading today.

Five

Norfolk Crescent to Upper Weston

NORFOLK CRESCENT *c.* 1903. Built between 1798 and 1812 and named after the Duke of Norfolk, a part of the crescent was bombed during the war and subsequently rebuilt as flats. Whilst the façade has been retained intact, except for several doorways, the rear, with modern concrete balconies, is most unsightly. The green would benefit from replacement railings to connect with the watchman's hut shown earlier.

NELSON PLACE WEST *c*. 1906. The watchman's box from the previous picture is on the left. One might be forgiven for wondering why traffic lights appear at such an early date, but these were used by the trams. Built in about 1800 and originally called Nelson Place, the West was added to avoid confusion with the rank of the same name near Cleveland Terrace. The whole row of houses have been restored and all the windows replaced with ones incorporating glazing bars.

CRESCENT GARDENS (C) 1905. This view can be seen from the end of Nile Street, which is approximately half way along Crescent Gardens. Built of varying styles and materials, they replaced various earlier dwellings in 1894. Today, many of them are used as guest houses.

UPPER BRISTOL ROAD (V) *c.* 1915. Albion Place dates from the late 1700s, with the Norfolk Arms on the right which opened as the Norfolk Tavern in 1856. The Western Dispensary adjoins the two-storey St George's Buildings. These are still intact, but the aforementioned premises were bombed and have been replaced by Hinton Garage.

VICTORIA SUSPENSION BRIDGE *c.* 1905. Erected by James Dredge, the owner of Norfolk Brewery and malthouse, this was the first of fifty or so built worldwide. Started in the summer of 1836, it carried a ½d. toll until June 1929. Here it is seen looking towards Bath. The gantry is a part of what was once Stothert & Pitt's works.

TENNYSON ROAD 1905. This view looks towards Victoria Park with Coronation Road on the right. The street lamps have gone, but the stone kerbs survive. Built in 1897, the houses are unaltered in appearance.

UPPER BRISTOL ROAD c. 1908. Windsor Villas on the right date from 1889. Harry Lay was a new and secondhand furniture dealer and cabinet maker (1906–52), but later became an undertaker too. His shop, Windsor House, is now a newsagents and the canopy has been replaced by a large fascia advertising the *Bath Chronicle*. The building that appears to be in the road was at the end of Windsor Bridge. A new road bridge now runs parallel to this. Finally, on the left, are the gardens of Locksbrook Place.

WESTON STATION 1905. Located in Ashley Avenue and built largely of pennant sandstone, it is today the Aquae Sulis Dental Practice. This view faces towards Saltford. The platform has gone, but more drastically the railway has been deeply excavated for a car park. In the distance is Station Road.

NEWBRIDGE ROAD (V) *c.* 1915. Located at the junction with the roads to Saltford and Kelston, the Weston Family Hotel was built in 1897 and has just been renamed the Sportsman. The houses on the right, now without the ivy, were built in about 1884.

NEWBRIDGE ROAD (F) 1909. Facing towards Saltford, Station Road is on the left and Chelsea Road on the right. The shop on the corner belonged to Frank Shorney, a greengrocer and gardener (1901–13). Richard Bennett had the Post Office (1906–24), which now has a letter box outside and Ward & Co., grocers (1900–11) now belongs to Andrew's Estate Agents. The last shop front was recently rebuilt after a road accident. A pelican crossing is located here in order to be able to cross the road today.

NEWBRIDGE ROAD (F) 1909. With only a tram in sight, this view facing towards Bath is opposite Horstmann's engineering factory, with Westbourne Terrace (erected 1889) on the right. The shrubs have now gone and only one roadside tree remains. As in many other locations, the tram wires have been superseded by masses of telegraph cables. The houses on the left are still the same, but the gardens have been turned into places to park the family car.

WESTON CUT *c.* 1890. The Dolphin Inn in River Terrace, Brassmill Lane is still in business today. Built mostly of lias, with some Bath stone, it now has a parapet wall at roof level. The stable block is still there, but the view has been obstructed by an extension to the public house. This picture has been taken from Weston Island, created when John Wood built the canal. The keystone of the bridge is dated 1728. Severely damaged during the blitz, the structure has since been restored.

NEWBRIDGE ROAD WEST (L) *c.* 1920. Viewed looking towards Bath, this is Addison Villas, put up in 1912. Note the Brooke's Dye Works laundry cart. Nowadays it would be eligible as a museum exhibit. The tree has been felled and replaced by a post box. Located on the corner of the road leading to Emmanuel Church, it is where Apsley Road was constructed a few years later. The break between the houses allows for Lyme Gardens to intervene.

EMMANUEL CHURCH, APSLEY ROAD (V) *c.* 1915. Erected in 1910, this corrugated iron structure has been replaced by a more substantial church built in reconstituted Bath stone. Nothing else in this picture remains, as the church has since been surrounded by housing.

NEWBRIDGE HILL 1905. This delightful view is from the junction of Combe Park looking in the direction of Kelston. The railings belong to the Weston Methodist Church and the houses on the left have since been obscured by trees and a garage. The right side is still much the same, but there are far fewer trees. A traffic island and street lights now adorn the road, which is an alternative route to Bristol.

COMBE PARK 1905. This faces towards Bath from the junction of Cedric Road and the main entrance of the Royal United Hospital. A pelican crossing is situated where the cart is parked and the gateway on the right now leads to the pharmacy stores.

WESTON ROAD 1905. Facing towards the village, on the left was the ornate entrance to Montrose (1871), now Mulberry House, a special needs centre. Beyond, a single gate post leads into Grove House (1897). On the right side, the hedge borders the grounds of Spring Grove, and the entrance leads to Summerfields, both built in 1865.

HIGH STREET, UPPER WESTON (F) 1907. The left-hand house belonged to James Greening, a carriage proprietor (1900–19) and is now the forecourt to Weston Garages. Straight ahead is the Infants' School, All Saints' Church Centre today. The war memorial stands where the water pump was located. Behind the Bath Cold Storage & Ice Co. Ltd. wagon was a grocers shop, in Crown Road run by George Little, which has now reverted to a private house.

POINTING'S BREWERY, TRAFALGAR ROAD c. 1912. Originally the Trafalgar Brewery, it came into the Pointing family in about 1854. From 1877 they also owned the Weston Brewery nearby. Although it closed in 1928, the family lived here until after the war. One of the few local breweries still standing, the house is unaltered, apart from the later Victorian bay window. The railings still survive as does the name along the front of the parapet. The malthouse has since lost the top storey.

Six

Widcombe to Combe Down

DOLEMEADS c. 1935. The river here is in major flood which all too frequently occurred, especially for this part of the city. This photograph may be of the floods in 1935. Ferry Place was on the left and St David's Place on the right. All were demolished in about 1938. The Mason's Arms (see page 15) in Ferry Place opened in 1857 and closed in 1914. In the background is St Matthew's Church.

SAMUEL ROGERS, CANAL BRIDGE, WIDCOMBE (DU) *c.* 1865. This picture shows the workforce in their work clothes. Samuel Rogers is recorded as having started in business in about 1819 in the Carriage Road, later moving to 7 Claverton Buildings. By 1854 this yard had opened, presumably by Samuel Rogers junior, and specialised in tombstones and monumental work. He died in 1881, when Edward Rogers succeeded him. Samuel Rogers may well be the second from the right with the bowler hat.

WIDCOMBE BAPTIST CHAPEL *c.* 1935. This part of the chapel was built in 1910, as witnessed by the date above the window and replaced some houses. The shop adjoining belonged to Charles Maslen, a boot repairer, and was part of Coburg Place. He worked here between 1932 and 1967, when soon after it was demolished for the chapel car park. On the right is Ebenezer Terrace or Chapel Place. The Ebenezer Chapel opened on 20 September 1821.

ST. MARK'S CHURCH
(D&D) *c.* 1863. In the
foreground on the right is
the end of St Mark's
Place West, built about
1840. St Mark's Church
is unaltered but is now
very blackened by air
pollution. To the left of
the church is the
graveyard, today devoid
of tombstones. The rear
of the houses in
Claverton Street
adjoining the churchyard
were Lyncombe Place.
Dating from 1843, they
were pulled down in
about 1965. In the
background can be seen
St James's Church. St
John's Roman Catholic
Church had yet to be
built.

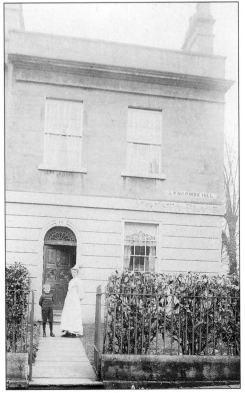

AUGUSTA PLACE, LYNCOMBE HILL
c. 1910. Built in about 1822, this is the house
at the top end of the rank. Still very similar to
the picture, the fence has been replaced by a
laurel bush and the front of the building is
now partly painted white. Although the lawn
has gone, it has been carefully relaid with
pennant slabs instead. For some strange reason
the two lines through the name of the
buildings have been removed.

WIDCOMBE PARADE 1926. The wine shop on the right closed only recently and beyond Millbrook Place, William Silcox & Sons owned the Rosemount Dairy. At the bottom of Widcombe Hill, now replaced by the hideous Widcombe Social Club and car park was Widcombe Wharf. Established in 1795, George Stockden was once a coal merchant here (1864–94).

CLAVERTON BUILDINGS 1904. On the left was Clifford Clement, a tobacconist and accountant (1901–4). The nearest shops as far as Spring Gardens Road were removed for a road scheme in 1970. The others have changed little apart from the Ram Tavern public house, which now has a large extension. The grassed area was Bolwell Buildings, demolished in 1893, a terrace of thirteen shops and houses. Next to this is Widcombe Parade, the end of which after many years of dereliction was rebuilt in the 1980s.

WIDCOMBE CRESCENT (W) c. 1908. Built in 1808 by Charles Harcourt Masters it is seen from the steps of Widcombe Terrace. The beautiful pineapple topped pillars and the ironwork arch are still there, but it holds an electric lamp these days. The railings on the right are surely a fine candidate for renewal. Surprisingly the pennant setts in the road are still in situ.

PRIOR PARK BUILDINGS (C) 1905. What an excellent idea to construct these houses alongside the mill stream. They were erected around 1825–6 and are still well screened from the road. Sadly the pennant sandstone paving slabs have been replaced by concrete ones. The mill stream on the left comes down from what was once Upper Widcombe Flour Mill. Recently vacated, this was previously a Citroën Garage.

PRIOR PARK VILLAS, PRIOR PARK ROAD c. 1915. This is a much altered bottom end of the Carriage Road, constructed by Ralph Allen for transporting stone from his quarries at Combe Down. These large villas were built in about 1846, which is presumably when the road was widened.

THE CARRIAGE ROAD (C) 1905. The lodge on the left is still identical, but has had a new wall built and gate fitted. The road, again a part of Allen's Carriage Road, now Ralph Allen Drive, has been substantially widened and abuts the right hand gate pillar. The gates beside the road lead into the Abbey cemetary. Unfortunately, the road widening has resulted in the felling of all the large trees seen here.

THE AVENUE, COMBE DOWN c. 1905. The Hadley Arms Hotel was named after the Hadley Estate. Farnham Flower, the landlord at this time had been the blacksmith at Newton St Loe from 1885. He took over the public house in 1901 and remained here for fourteen years. Today all the decorated areas of the façade have been painted over in green. The Bath Brewery Ltd. was taken over by George's Bristol Brewery in 1923.

NORTH ROAD, COMBE DOWN c. 1905. A fairly active scene at Raby Place. The first shop has since been returned to private use and has a bow fronted window today. The second has a large extension in the garden and has also closed. The public house opened as the The Crown Inn in 1849 and became the Three Crowns Inn by 1858. William Miles was the landlord (1884–1926), a plumber and also a publisher of post cards of Combe Down. The large dividing wall has been cut down and the public house closed in 1963.

RAINBOW WOODS, COMBE DOWN (V) c. 1915. This popular location has fared very badly in recent years. Firstly by the great storm in January 1990, which destroyed great swathes of trees. Soon after, an encampment by a large group of travellers damaged the land still further. If that was not enough, it is the most likely future site for the concrete batching plant that will be needed should the quarries below Combe Down be infilled.

RICHARDSON AVENUE, COMBE DOWN c. 1914. Started in 1907, the street was renamed The Firs in 1926. Sadly the trees on the side of the road have gone. This view shows James Dolman's shop on the end of the terrace. A dairyman, he was here from 1931 until 1938, but nowadays this shop has been transformed into a veterinary surgery. In the distance is a Clement-Bayard delivery van. It was registered in Bristol as AE 2572 and belonged to James Fortt's confectionary business in Green Street.

CHURCH ROAD, COMBE DOWN (V) c. 1915. The rank of houses, running into the distance, was known as De Montalt Place and was originally built to house Ralph Allen's quarrymen. The house with the large pitched roof on the left, called Lonsdale, is considerably more modern. On the right is Holy Trinity Church, the foundation stone of which was laid on 22 May 1832.

CHURCH ROAD, COMBE DOWN 1910. This view is from further along the road near Tyning Road. The large house nearest is known as Combe Lodge. For some reason the railings still survive along a part of its frontage. The house cannot be seen any more at this spot as a large tree now obscures the view. Since this photograph was taken the vegetation behind the wall on the right has been removed. Two tracks lead from this road into the old quarry workings, mostly abandoned by 1850.

MIDFORD ROAD, COMBE DOWN (DA) c. 1940. This is the Cross Keys Hotel at the junction with the road to Southstoke. Ernest Weaver, the landlord, succeeded his son William in 1914. Still in operation today, it hasn't really altered since this time. Just visible on the left is one of the many guide posts erected by Somerset County Council in the mid 1930s. This one is still here, but as is so often the case it now has an arm missing. The lone car in the distance is a Jaguar SS100.

Seven

Twerton on Avon
to Odd Down

NEWTON ROAD, TWERTON 1910. This is the top of How Hill, just after the junction with Watery Lane. The drive to Pool Meade is on the left, which was home to the Carr family from 1876 to 1931, owners of Twerton mills. The left side of the lane is still the same, but the right side has been developed with many modern homes.

HIGH STREET, TWERTON 1910. Henry Hicks owned the Old Crown Inn from 1907–10. Next door was the Twerton Club and Institute, but where the wall is situated, there is now a dreadful reconstituted stone house. The enamelled signs on the end of Tom Powell's (1907–26) bakery have long gone, as has the wall in front of the shop. The houses on the far left are Chilcott's Cottages. The canopy and fence outside the left hand shop are no more and the railway footbridge has also gone.

HIGH STREET, TWERTON 1910. The shop on the corner of Shophouse Lane belonging to William Lawrence, a newsagent from 1911, was bombed on 16 January 1941 and William Wiltshire's grocery store to the left of the lane (1908–15) was demolished in 1932. Now renamed Shophouse Road, this area looks very untidy. The White Hart Brewery (c. 1846–97) name can still just be seen on the end wall to the right of the newsagents. The end pair of matching houses on the right have also been taken down.

TWERTON STATION *c.* 1910. This view from the trackbed is facing in the direction of Bath. The station opened in 1840, but closed in 1917 to be replaced by one in Oldfield Park. Note the many enamelled advertising signs on the fence, once so common a sight, but highly collectable these days.

TWERTON STATION (W) *c.* 1908. As well as the station, the Railway Inn (1894–1940), later the Railway Hotel, has gone. To the right is Bence's Yard which led to the Royal Old Ferry. Later it became Old Ferry Road. The shop on the corner still stands, occupied by Clark Copiers. On the right side of the road were Railway Buildings, the last of which were taken down in 1994. Note the GWR steam carriage.

THE ROYAL OLD FERRY, TWERTON *c.* 1906. This was the last ferry to work the River Avon and closed on 7 April 1906. The malthouse next door was located just off of Fielding's Buildings and behind was another near to the Seven Stars public house.

TWERTON LOWER MILLS *c.* 1890. Created by John Wood's canal in 1727, the end of Dutch Island can just be seen to the left of the old weir. Twerton Lower Mills are to the right and rear. Owned by W. & R. Cook Ltd from 1891, they were pulled down in 1965. To the left of this mill is Woodland Buildings, also no longer existing.

AVON BUILDINGS, WEST TWERTON *c.* 1905. The Seven Stars has lost its pictorial sign and the Golden Fleece Brewery, originally the Fleece, is no longer a brewery. The shop front has been replaced by a window and is now a part of the pub. The adjoining houses and malthouse have been demolished and converted into garages.

ALBANY ROAD, WEST TWERTON (V) *c.* 1915. Built in 1898 and looking towards Lansdown View, the road now continues back beyond where the photographer was standing. The brick-built factory was the Albany Works of F. Chivers & Co., soap manufacturers.

CHARLTON BUILDINGS, WEST TWERTON (W) *c.* 1908. On the left is Vernon Terrace, built in 1885. Charlton Buildings only came about in 1891 as a combination of various cottages and houses. Now mostly of industrial use, including Herman Miller Ltd. and Hygate Transmissions Ltd., this area has fallen into an embarrassing mess.

SOUTH VIEW ROAD, EAST TWERTON 1897. Started in 1881, the south side was still incomplete in 1885. Facing away from Brook Road, here we see Queen Victoria's Diamond Jubilee being celebrated on 22 June 1897.

WEST AVENUE, SOUTH TWERTON *c.* 1915. This street dates from 1889. William Powell, furniture remover (1912–37) occupied the house on the left. Note the Twerton Co-operative Society Ltd. handcart with loaves of bread sticking out of the top.

MILLMEAD ROAD, SOUTH TWERTON 1905. Looking towards Lyndhurst Road, the wall on the left now has a fence on top and the lamp outside the Victoria Hotel has gone. Built in 1897, Charles Davis (1898–1906) was the landlord at the time. The dairy run by Ebenezer Chesterman (1898–1907) has reverted to private use.

93

RINGWOOD ROAD, SOUTH TWERTON *c.* 1908. Started in 1897, here we are looking uphill with Lyndhurst Road on the left. A row of fir trees now blocks the view on the left hand side. The removal of the railings has resulted in a variety of styles of reconstituted stone walls taking their place. The pleasingly designed lamp column on the right has now been exchanged for a concrete one and the large chimney at the top corner of the street no longer cuts the skyline.

SOUTH TWERTON SCHOOLS, LYMORE AVENUE 1905. Built in 1893 and still in use today, I would imagine that these must be some of the pupils posing in front of the school. It is an unusual design with its copper-roofed tower on the corner topped by a cockerel weather vane.

THE TRIANGLE, SOUTH TWERTON (W) *c.* 1906. Construction started in 1893 and took several years to finish. The clock tower central to the Oldfield Park Baptist Church has gone. Triangle Villas are just visible on the left. What is now called Triangle East can be seen on the right and Triangle North beyond. These houses were built largely of pennant sandstone and remain unchanged, although the ivy has since been killed off.

OLDFIELD PARK BAPTIST CHURCH 1917. Here we can see the church looking from the end of Triangle East. Today, the doors have been renewed and the sign board has gone. The railings have been replaced by a rather unsightly chain link fence and the arch over the gateway has gone.

MOORLAND ROAD, SOUTH TWERTON (W) *c.* 1908. Taken from the junction of Crandale and Maybrick Roads, the right-hand shop was owned by Walter Malcombe, a bootmaker (1894–1932). The post office and grocers shop on the left was bombed in 1942, as well as the Livingstone Hotel which was rebuilt here in 1965, with ugly glass block windows.

MOORLAND ROAD, SOUTH TWERTON *c.* 1927. This was the front of Smith & Bottrill, watchmakers. Established in 1913, they were only here for a year or two. Now fitted with a modern shop front it is occupied by the Victoria Wine Company.

VICTORIA BUILDINGS, EAST TWERTON 1905. This excellent photograph was taken from the bottom of Brougham Hayes. The three-storey Longmead Buildings (built *c.* 1846) were later incorporated into Victoria Buildings (started 1861). Now canopyless, were James Nelson & Sons Ltd., butchers, and the Victoria Dining and Refreshment Rooms next door.

WESTMORELAND TERRACE, LOWER BRISTOL ROAD 1905. Built in 1875, today many of these shops have declined. Beside the newsagents, 'Use Hearse's Embrocation' is still visible on top of Frederick Hearse's Westmoreland Tea Warehouse (1876–1925).

VIEW FROM BEECHEN CLIFF *c.* 1865. The brewhouse of Holloway Brewery in Paradise Row has been removed and an extension is about to be added to Paradise House. This and the brewery were owned by John Hibbard (*c.* 1826–1889). The house in the foreground was Magdalen Cottage, now just a ruin. The long clean building is the Newark Foundry of Stothert & Pitt (1857) and to its right was the Bell Inn and brewery, demolished in 1896. Behind the foundry can be seen the two wings of Green Park Buildings.

BLOOMFIELD AVENUE (W) c. 1905. Before this area was developed it was previously occupied by a nursery. The houses were erected in 1893. The west side of the avenue consists of an interesting variety of building styles and materials. On the right, a large wall has replaced the fence and beyond the last house on the left is a large open green, containing a tennis court.

HAYESFIELD TERRACE, WELLS ROAD c. 1908. Built in 1896, the bank and the end of the terrace next to Bruton Avenue were rebuilt following bomb damage. This included Edward Batten's grocery shop at Dorset House (1907–42) on the left, now a post office. The same shop front has been moved next door. To its right, were Davies & John, chemists, a branch of the business in Old Bond Street. The tree outside the house besides Holloway's the butchers is now taller than the house itself.

SHAKESPEARE AVENUE (W) *c.* 1908. Started in 1899, this is one of the streets in the vicinity known unofficially as Poet's Corner. The United Methodist Church is on the left and trees still line the roadside to this day.

SHAKESPEARE AVENUE 1905. This is the left side of the upper part of the avenue, leading into Alexandra Park. Many of the decorative branched gables are missing from the houses now. As opposed to the lower part of the road seen above, new trees have been planted on the road side.

KIPLING AVENUE *c.* 1926. Located slightly further along the Wells Road from Bath these terraces weren't started until 1902. Note the Twerton Co-operative Society milk cart standing in the middle of the street. Today, with all the parked cars and passing traffic, this would no longer be possible.

OLD WELLS ROAD *c.* 1926. Taken from Entry Hill Drive, modern houses now occupy the foreground and valley bottom. The tall rank on the left is Devonshire Terrace, with Terrace Vale below. The group of buildings in the valley at the junction of Lynbrook Lane were once a smithy. There is an unattractive reconstituted stone house here now. The church spire in the background belongs to St Luke's Church and further to the right is Claverton View.

FROME ROAD, ODD DOWN (L) *c.* 1920. This is the junction with Bloomfield Road, commonly known as Noad's Corner. Nearest is Odd Down Post Office, grocery store (1895–date) and public house. It was called, variously, the Rising Sun and Rising Star until its closure in 1909. Today, the lamp has gone, plate glass windows have been fitted, a large fascia stretches across the shop front and it has had another shop added beside it. There are still only these four houses further along the road.

BELLEVUE TERRACE, ODD DOWN (L) *c.* 1920. Built in 1904, this terrace is now a part of Oolite Road. On the right, new houses have been built surrounding the ones seen here, but as has so often occurred, they have been unfittingly made of reconstituted stone. The road has since been properly made up, yet there are still a few streets around Bath like this today!

Eight

The Surrounding Villages

ST MARY MAGDALENE CHURCH, LANGRIDGE (V) *c*. 1915. This tiny church is of considerable age. It has a Norman doorway and a short square Norman tower. The chancel was restored by Davis in 1872. Behind the building are some hidden farm buildings, otherwise it is quite a remote location. The fir tree in the graveyard is not there any more and a doorway has been added to this side to the building.

ALL SAINTS CHURCH, WOOLLEY, APRIL 1874. This more recent church was built by John Wood the Younger in 1761. The tree blocking its view here has since matured and now completely obscures this view. A different gate has been fitted to the churchyard and a George V post box has been installed in the wall alongside it.

ST. MARY THE VIRGIN CHURCH, CHARLCOMBE (DU) *c.* 1865. Restored in 1857, the church dates from the Norman period, but the site dates back to Saxon times. The nave and chancel were restored in 1861, just a few years earlier than this photograph. The cross on the gable end has gone and a new entrance porch has been constructed. Also the well constructed boundary wall was replaced by railings, which have also been taken away. The lane is now a mixed surface of tarmacadam and grass.

104

GLOUCESTER BUILDINGS, LOWER SWAINSWICK *c.* 1906. It now stands all alone. This was once the end property in a row of nineteen houses originally called Lower Gloucester Buildings, built in about 1850. The remainder were pulled down in the 1970s. It has lost its chimney pots, unsightly rectangular windows adorn the ground floor and the garden has a large driveway ramped across it. Altogether this area is now only a shadow of its past.

BAILBROOK *c.* 1920. The three-storey house on the right has been pulled down along with the curved wall. The buildings in the foreground were a rank of four terraced houses demolished probably in the 1950s. A detached house stands here today. This view is taken immediately adjacent to the boundary of the recently opened Swainswick Bypass. The brick building in the centre is Bailbrook School.

BAILBROOK BUILDINGS *c.* 1920. Bailbrook's corrugated iron chapel is still with us, but has since lost its bell tower. The terrace was built about 1850. Today many of the garden walls have deteriorated and some of the houses are now painted as well as having porches added. The second from the last of the lower rank has been fitted with dormer windows thus spoiling the integrity of the rank. Note the patterns scratched on the garden wall and the tall radio masts outside two of the houses.

BATHEASTON MILL AND BATHAMPTON BRIDGE (LL) 1905. Batheaston Flour Mills were rebuilt in 1844 from an earlier structure, but were sadly burnt down on 14 November 1909. The remains were later converted into a restaurant and hotel. The bridge was built in 1872 to replace an ancient ferry that previously crossed here.

HIGH STREET, BATHEASTON c. 1908. Avondale Garage has replaced Hewlett & Appleby, plumbers and contractors (1901–14), but worst of all, the Lamb and Flag public house was pulled down in about 1970 for car parking. Between them is Avoncliffe, which has recently been superbly restored.

GEORGE & DRAGON, STAMBRIDGE PLACE, BATHEASTON c. 1910. Albert Bevan, a farmer, was the landlord at this time. Once a home brew pub, after many refits, it has been greatly enlarged and has little character remaining.

FIVEWAYS, BATHEASTON *c.* 1906. This is definitely not Bathampton. Fosse Lane passes to the left of the central cottage and Bannerdown Road to the right. Bundy & Taylor's workshop on the left has been rebuilt with the pitched roof at right angles to that in the picture and the line of cottages on the right of Fosse Lane have all gone. Only the upper one remained by 1932 and that went soon after 1968. The large house beyond is Fosse Cottage, but today is totally obscured by trees.

THE MEAD, ST. CATHERINE'S (DA) *c.* 1935. This rural scene with the smoke rising from the chimney is so characteristic of the countryside around Bath. For about fifty years this was home to the once popular tea gardens, which have recently closed. Very little has changed here, apart from the loss of the greenhouses.

108

ST. CATHERINE'S VALLEY 1921. This view of the winding lane and valley remain almost timeless. The valley with its derelict mills and old farms is one of my favourite areas to visit locally, never more so than on a hot summer's day. Only the metalled surface of the road has modernised the setting.

KINGSLEIGH GARDENS, BATHFORD (DA) *c.* 1935. Taken from the now non-existent platform of Bathford railway station, these houses were built in 1926. The gardens belonging to the left three have recently been cut back due to the works associated with the construction of the Batheaston Bypass. A new garage has been added to the middle house and the trees have matured considerably since this shot was taken.

KINGSLEIGH GARAGE, BATHFORD c. 1935. Opened in 1929 by Benjamin Makin, motor engineer, it is hard to recognise this building any more. Two large wings have been added and the central door is an entrance to the office. Most of all a wide fascia extends the full length of the building naming the owners, Dunsford Land Rovers.

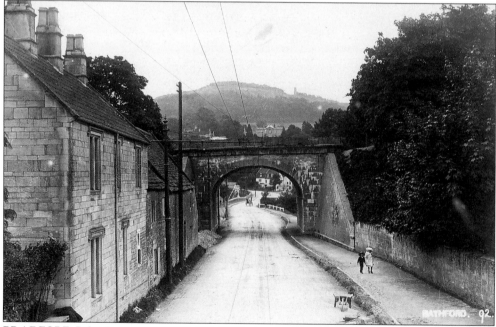

BRADFORD ROAD, BATHFORD (C) 1905. A roundabout was built here in 1979 and as a result Bridge Farm, later Bridge Farm Garage, on the left was taken down. The Quaker burial ground on the right has recently been removed as a part of the new works for the Batheaston Bypass.

VIEW OF BATHFORD (DU) *c.* 1865. The ford across the By Brook is now all but gone and the Crown Inn belonged to Jeanette Grist. Many trees have grown since, notably on Farleigh Down. Eagle House is the large building prominently situated behind the inn. The tablet on the side of Bathford Bridge explains that it was built in 1665.

CROWN INN, BATHFORD *c.* 1910. Rebuilt in 1904, it has since lost the fencing and other paraphernalia. Frederick Lavington was the landlord, also a farmer and caterer (1883–1926) and later a haulier. His wife continued to run the inn until 1932.

BATHFORD HILL (L) *c.* 1920. Looking down the hill, on the left beside the steps can be seen the grocery store belonging to Mrs C. Whiteley (1920–8). A shop as far back as at least 1854, it was previously owned by the Newman family, but after Mrs Whiteley left it became a private residence. On the right behind the wall are the well-wooded grounds of Whitehaven, once known as Titan Barrow.

CHURCH STREET, BATHFORD (V) *c.* 1915. This quiet village street is not very different today, apart from the line of parked cars. The water outlet may have gone, but the rag stone footway still survives. Beyond the garden walls, the single storey building was at this time the Bathford Post Office, but is today used as a garage.

THE NEW INN, BATHFORD (V) *c.* 1915. This inn was first recorded in 1733. On closing in 1994 it was transformed into the village post office. The upper windows, blocked for many years, presumably as a result of the window tax, have lately been reopened. On the left, with the canopy, was Arthur Maslen's grocery store (1892–1916), also closed today.

UPPER STORES, HIGH STREET, BATHFORD *c.* 1908. This shop was owned by Albert Brooke, grocer and baker (1897–1912) and then by Mrs Brooke until 1918. The windows have now been enlarged with plate glass, which do little justice to the store.

VIEW FROM THE HOLLOW *c.* 1907. This is taken from the corner of the extremely steep lane to Monkton Farleigh. The sloping terrace of houses on the right are Woodland Place and were built in about 1883. Next to them is a track which passes through a stile and into the field. Known as Dovers Lane, it is quite possibly an old Roman road. The large tree in the field was felled in the early 1970s when much of the woods above Bathford were cleared.

KINGSDOWN (DA) *c.* 1935. No longer a grassy bank. All the trees have gone and the cottages have undergone many changes since this time. The lean-to and the garage, including the wall behind, have been taken away. Where the garage once stood, an extension has taken its place on the front of Jessamine Cottage and in the background Laurel Cottage has had a large extension added. Kingsdown Post Office was also situated here, but has long been closed.

MONKTON FARLEIGH (W) *c.* 1908. The entrance to St Peter's Church can be seen on the right. Today the lamp as well as the trees have all gone. The first house on the left is Church Cottage. Unlike Church Street in Bathford the stone footway has gone.

FARLEIGH WICK (W) *c.* 1905. This is one of six Milnes Daimler buses delivered in August 1905. A road improvement here in the 1980s has altered the road considerably. The raised pavement beyond the Fox and Hounds public house is no longer there and Midway Cottage this side of the public house has been rebuilt, infilling a gap after many years.

GATE HOUSE, WARLEIGH MANOR c. 1908. This pretty little building is sited opposite the entrance to Warleigh Manor on approaching from Bathford. Happily it is now inhabited again after having been empty for many years. The lane continues on towards Conkwell after rising steeply through Warleigh Wood.

WARLEIGH LANE c. 1907. This delightful view of the lane was taken as it passes by Warleigh Manor. The road has now been tarmacadamed and these large trees still fill the valley side. Perhaps the most depressing feature since the last member of the Skrine family passed away, is the way that long stretches of boundary walling have been allowed to crumble away on so much of this estate.

FERRY COTTAGE, WARLEIGH c. 1908.
The two cottages are now occupied as one and
may date back to the seventeenth century.
When the ferry was operating, a bell system was
used to summon the ferryman from this house
to bring people across from the island at
Claverton. Today there are two small timber
footbridges crossing to the island. For a while
there was a tea gardens here and a large copper
caldron was used for boiling the water.

WARLEIGH FERRY c. 1908. Taken on a cold winter's day, we can just see the boat on the
Warleigh side of the river. Recorded as having been in existence for at least 250 years, use of the
ferry died out in the 1950s. It cost 2d. to cross the river and George Moulder was the last
ferryman. An earlier ferryman was Charles Jones, who carried out this task for forty two years
until he died in 1932, aged eighty eight.

CONKWELL *c.* 1905. This is the bottom of the village, facing towards Winsley. The central building is the tea rooms and the sign reads 'Tea parties accommodated – ginger beer etc.'. Run by Mrs E. Dallimore (1886–1906), it was reopened in 1921 for many more years of use. The attached single storey building was replaced soon after by a large extension. The building behind the well is inscribed as having been built in 1876 and in the foreground on the right is a part of Spring Cottage.

THE WISHING WELL, CONKWELL (W) *c.* 1923. This notable feature of the village is now protected by ugly steel railings. No water comes from the doorway at the end any more, but now runs down the left side of the path, having been piped at some time in the past. The cottage in the background is known as Cromwells Rest, no doubt relating to the English Civil War, when an army of men passed through this area prior to amassing for the Battle of Lansdown.

THE OLD TURNPIKE ROAD, BATHAMPTON *c.* 1908. The new road from Bathwick to Limpley Stoke was opened in 1835 and curves away to the right, whist the village road falls away to the left. This view has changed dramatically, as the road is now much wider and has a layby beyond the junction. There are now street lights, telegraph poles, road signs, white lines, footways, and a constant stream of traffic. On the right many houses have been built. The water trough and the guide post have long gone.

THE KENNET AND AVON CANAL, BATHAMPTON (C) 1905. The George Inn was probably here long before the arrival of the canal. The inn sign for O.J. Saunders (1894–1910) is still here today, along with another to its right. The canal has returned to life again, with barges using it all year around. The Old Mill, a part of Harbutt's Plasticine factory, was replaced after a fire in 1963. With the closure of the factory, housing has taken its place here as well as behind Chapel Row, next to the mill.

HAMPTON DOWN *c*. 1908. Now much more vegetated, here we can see evidence of stone quarrying. Ralph Allen took over existing workings, but not for very long. It was only when the canal arrived that quarrying extended underground on a large scale. A major news story occurred here in September 1893 when the skeleton of a young woman was found in one of the old workings. Presumed murdered, witnesses reported finding articles of clothing nearby, about two years prior to the discovery.

CLAVERTON (L) *c*. 1920. This building on the right is known as Farleigh Cottage and is now bounded by a wall. The three-storey building adjoining it is unsurprisingly known as Tower House. The barns belonging to the old farm in the background have since been converted as dwellings.

MONKTON COMBE SCHOOL *c.* 1905. This is the oldest part of Monkton Combe School and has the inscription TC 1714 on one of the gables. The shutters have gone as has the blocked up window next to the door. The far building has been replaced by a well-designed three-storey stone structure. Today a two-storey extension links the two buildings, criminally destroying the full facade of the earlier building.

MILL ROAD, MONKTON COMBE *c.* 1905. The Somerset Coal Canal has been and gone and so has the Camerton and Limpley Stoke Railway, built on the line of the old canal. Apart from Martin Cottage on the right which has had a two-storey extension tacked on the front, nothing else in this picture remains. With new housing on the left, comprising various materials and styles, this area is a sorry sight today when compared with the pleasant scene in the photograph.

LIMPLEY STOKE 1910. This fine view shows the post office on the right next to Berkeley Cottage which was run by W. Weston (1884–1914). The delightful Hop Pole Inn, is mainly unaltered, apart from a large illuminated Courage sign over the doorway.

HYDRO, LIMPLEY STOKE *c.* 1909. Constructed in about 1865 as the West of England Hydropathic Establishment, it later became a hydro-hotel. In business today as the Limpley Stoke Hotel, it is still very sumptuous inside. The main building is as pictured here, although there have been many additions to the rear.

LIMPLEY STOKE STATION (W) *c.* 1923. Hardly recognisable anymore, the inn car park is where the stone stacking yard was. The signal box, water tower, platforms, and signal have all been swept away. Clare Cottage can be seen behind the stacked stone.

MIDFORD *c.* 1905. The embankment of the Somerset and Dorset Railway is now tree covered, blocking this view today. The Camerton and Limpley Stoke Railway has yet to pass through the viaduct and the Somerset Coal Canal bridge can be seen just in front of the cottages on Midford Hill. Only the left one of the pair of cottages survives.

MIDFORD (DA) *c.* 1935. This view of the village is facing in the direction of Hinton Charterhouse and has been taken from the railway station. The Camerton and Limpley Stoke Railway crosses the road in the distance. This closed in the 1950s and the bridge no longer spans the road. Note the steam roller in front, possibly having surfaced the road for the first time.

SOMERSET COAL CANAL, MIDFORD *c.* 1907. This is the canal much as it appears today. Built in 1794, it was abandoned in 1898 following many years of competition from the Great Western Railway who eventually became its owners.

SOUTH STOKE (L) *c.* 1920. This photograph taken just above the Pack Horse Inn is so full of character. The cottage has changed greatly today. The creeper has been removed, the doorway blocked up, the windows altered and the shutters taken off. The stone gutter in the road has also gone, as has the stone slab at the threshold.

ENGLISHCOMBE 1904. Looking from Englishbatch, the post office was occupied by Joseph Love. Closed in 1918, it is now known as Crossways House. On the left are Duchy Villas, rebuilt following a fire a few years earlier. Beyond this house was the forge and through the trees is Jasmine Cottage. This has since been demolished. The skyline has since been filled with housing to the left of Twerton Round Hill.

CHAVE'S TEA GARDENS, ENGLISHCOMBE *c.* 1910. Mrs Chave was a carriage proprietress and ran the tea gardens from 1905 until 1916. Following this, it reverted to being a farmhouse. These days it is known as Blake's Farm and appears somewhat less inviting than when seen here, as the garden has lost the benches and flower beds.

NEWTON ST. LOE *c.* 1926. This view is taken from the church gates. Many of the properties here are built of lias limestone. A sundial on the house on the left is inscribed HWH 1715. Opposite is the Free School, built by Richard James of Stowey in 1698 and restored in 1911. The large tree on the right has since been felled for an extension to the school. The small island at the junction has disappeared and the stone footway has been shortened. Straight ahead can be seen the Old Rectory.

NEWTON PARK (L) *c.* 1920. Newton House was built for Joseph Langton between 1762 and 1765. This later became the home of the Gore-Langton family, but is now the Bath College of Higher Education training faculty. As a Grade One listed building this Georgian masterpiece still looks like this today. Just to set it off, a sundial has been placed in the middle of the grass island.

ST NICHOLAS CHURCH, KELSTON (L) *c. 1920*. This church has altered very little to this day. Part of the nave is semi-Norman and the chancel arch is Early English.

NORTH STOKE *c. 1907*. This view of the village has been taken from the top of the lane. With Lansdown behind the camera and facing south from the little church, Manor Farm is on the right with Manor House Farm in the background.